FIGURE SKATING
FOR FUN!

By Jen Jones

Content Adviser: Jennifer Elia, Veteran Figure Skater, Pasadena, California
Reading Adviser: Frances J. Bonacci, Ed.D., Reading Specialist, Cambridge, Massachusetts

COMPASS POINT BOOKS
MINNEAPOLIS, MINNESOTA

Compass Point Books
3109 West 50th Street, #115
Minneapolis, MN 55410

Visit Compass Point Books on the Internet at www.compasspointbooks.com
or e-mail your request to custserv@compasspointbooks.com

Photographs ©: Che jie/ImagineChina/Icon SMI, front cover (left), 29 (left); Photodisc, front cover (right) 11 (top), 19 (right), 42 (center, right); Krista Hicks Benson/Icon SMI, 4-5, 24-25; Istockphoto, 7; Chris Barry/Action Plus/Icon SMI, 8-9; Corel, 10, 27, 29 (right), 30, 34-35, 42, 43 (left, right), 44, 45, 47; Photos.com, 11 (bottom); AP Wide World Photos, 12-13, 14-15, 20-21, 22-23, 36, 37, 38-39; Steve Bardens/Action Plus/Icon SMI, 16-17; Don Mason/Corbis, 18-19 (center); Phillipe Millereau/DDPI/Icon SMI, 31; Stan Liu/Icon SMI, 32-33; David Seelig/Icon SMI, 40-41; Mario Tama/Getty Images, 42–43 (bottom spread).

Editors: Deb Berry and Aubrey Whitten/Bill SMITH STUDIO; and Shelly Lyons
Designer/Page Production: Geron Hoy, Kavita Ramchandran, Sinae Sohn, Marina Terletsky, and Brock Waldron/Bill SMITH STUDIO
Photo Researcher: Jacqueline Lissy Brustein, Scott Rosen, and Allison Smith/Bill SMITH STUDIO
Art Director: Jaime Martens
Creative Director: Keith Griffin
Editorial Director: Carol Jones
Managing Editor: Catherine Neitge

Library of Congress Cataloging-in-Publication Data

Jones, Jen, 1976-
  Figure skating for fun! / by Jen Jones.
     p. cm. -- (For fun!)
  Includes bibliographical references and index.
  ISBN 0-7565-1679-X (hard cover)
  1. Figure skating--Juvenile literature. I. Title. II. Series.
  GV850.223.J65 2006
  796.91'2--dc22
                          2005030279

Printed in the United States of America.

Table of Contents

Note: In this book, there are two kinds of vocabulary words. Figure Skating Words to Know are words specific to figure skating. They are defined on page 46. Other Words to Know are helpful words that aren't related only to figure skating. These are defined on page 47.

The Ice Age

Much like gymnastics, figure skating requires a high amount of athletic ability, style, and grace. Many professional skaters say that from the time they tried on their first pair of skates, they were hooked. It's easy to see why skating is so much fun to watch. The sport combines elements of dance with fast-paced skating and complicated turns, jumps, and lifts.

In ice rinks around the world, new skaters hit the ice for the first time every day. Some of them hope to become famous; others just take personal enjoyment in the exercise and excitement the sport provides. Although figure skating is a lot of fun, it's not 100 percent glamour. Those who are serious

about learning are subject to lots of early morning practices, hours spent in the brisk cold, and the risk of painful falls while learning new skills. But ask skaters who have been through it, and they'll probably tell you it's all worth it!

Jackson Haines

Known in some circles as the father of figure skating, this English skater shunned the stiff, rigid style of that time to create a stylish dance on the ice. Born in 1840, he was the first person to skate with musical accompaniment. Haines staged skating exhibitions around the world and became an international celebrity for his "Viennese style" of skating.

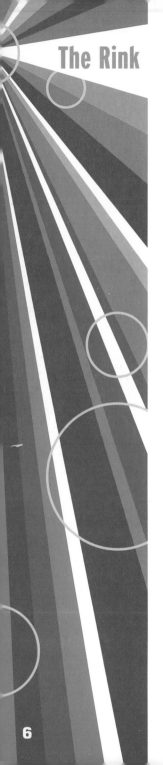

Get to Know the Ice

An ice rink is like your own personal winter wonderland. While the air is brisk inside the rink, it's not too chilly. The air temperature in most rinks is about 50 degrees Fahrenheit (10 degrees Celsius). (That's not counting the body heat you'll build up while practicing!)

So how does the ice stay solid? A complex system underneath the ice is constantly at work for that very purpose. Underground refrigeration systems pump out thousands of gallons of chilled water through steel pipes. Those pipes then distribute the water to form ice on a large concrete slab, which is kept below freezing temperature.

Although skating rinks range in size, a "regulation-size" indoor rink measures 200 feet (61 meters) long and 85 feet (26 meters) wide. If a rink is regulation-sized, it meets the standards of the National Hockey League and is more attractive to competitive skaters and hockey players.

Zooming Zamboni

With so many skaters on the ice throughout the day, it becomes necessary for a Zamboni machine to shave layers off the ice regularly. This keeps the ice's smooth surface intact. Zambonis weigh about 6,480 pounds (2,916 kilograms) and require 15 to 30 minutes to clean the ice efficiently.

The Insider's Guide to the Ice

Figure skating is a unique hybrid of ice skating, ballet, and acrobatics. Many people adopt skating as a hobby or as a way of staying in shape, while others hope to become professional or competitive figure skaters. Those who work toward greatness in figure skating have a world of opportunity open to them, from competitions to exhibitions, to professional career paths.

Although traditionally viewed as a winter sport, skating opportunities are available on a year-round basis. In the wintertime, skaters are able to take advantage of both indoor and outdoor ice arenas. Once they freeze over, lakes and other natural water areas are transformed into public ice rinks. (When skating outdoors, pay attention to safety warnings and always make sure there is supervision!) In warmer times of the year, skating enthusiasts can turn to indoor ice rinks to get their fix.

A Star Sport

There is no doubt that skating has touched the lives of many. Its popularity is proven in that it is one of the highest rated televised Olympic sports. Thousands of singles and pairs compete annually in local, regional, national, and international competitions.

Fitting Fashion

The most important part of any skating ensemble is, of course, the skates! Although it can be expensive to buy skates that are just the right size and fit, it's a smart move in protecting your most valuable skating asset: your feet. Buying quality skates makes a big difference in comfort and mobility on the ice.

When suiting up to go skating, you should wear clothes that are warm and easy to move around in. For practice, girls normally layer sweatshirts over leotards with skirts and tights, and boys usually pair T-shirts with sweatpants or stretch pants. Wearing gloves will shield your hands from the cold ice when you take a spill.

An ice skate is made up of a leather boot and a steel blade, which are normally sold separately. When not on the ice, it's important to keep your blades dry to prevent rusting and to have them sharpened regularly. (Blade protectors, or skate guards, are also available to keep the blades in good shape.)

Trusty Tips for Choosing Skates

The right skates will fit snugly around your foot and provide strong support for your ankles. (The size should be a half- to a full-size smaller than your normal shoe size.)

And for Beginners

Whether you live in a big city or small town, you're likely to be able to find an ice rink within driving distance. Web sites on skating or the local phonebook will help you find the rink nearest to your location. At the rink, you'll be able to take advantage of skating classes as well as public sessions where you can practice.

For those just starting out, inexpensive group "Learn to Skate" classes and camps are a great beginning point. Beginner (or alpha) groups focus on skills such as gliding, stops, dips, and other basics. As you progress through the different skill levels, you can take advanced group classes that focus on more challenging moves.

Axel Paulsen

If Axel Paulsen's name sounds familiar, it's because he invented the popular "Axel" jump of modern figure skating. In 1882, Paulsen placed third in the first international skating tournament. Although he didn't win, he was forever remembered for the daring jump he performed, which used one-and-a-half revolutions in the air.

Getting Limber

Like other sports, figure skating is physically demanding. Warming up your body before any skating session is crucial; otherwise, you may get hurt when attempting even the simplest skills. It'll also rev up your body temperature before you hit the cold!

Although it's important to do exercises like arm circles and neck rolls, the most important body parts to stretch before skating are your hips, lower back, and legs. They contribute to your power to jump, spin, and push off the ice with ease. The following are some effective stretches to work these muscles:

Hamstring Stretch: While standing, lift one foot and bend your other leg beneath you. Keep your knees close together, grab your lifted foot, and pull it toward your back. Hold the pose as long as you can, using something for balance if necessary. Repeat on the other side.

Hip Rotations: Stand with your hands on your hips and feet apart. Lean over to the left while pushing your hips to the right, then lean forward while pushing your hips back, and so on until you've made a complete circle with your upper body. Hold each stretch for several seconds.

On the Edge

Skaters live on the edge. After all, the foundation of every skating maneuver lies within the edges of your skate blades. Whether you're performing a simple forward glide or complicated jump, you'll need to use the inside edge, outside edge, or both edges to push off the ice.

The "inside edges" of your skates are between your feet, facing inward, and the "outside edges" are on the opposite side, facing away from your body. There is a hollow area that separates the two edges, which you can see if you turn your skates upside down. The front ends of your skates also have toe picks, which are ridges that propel skaters into the air for jumps and flips.

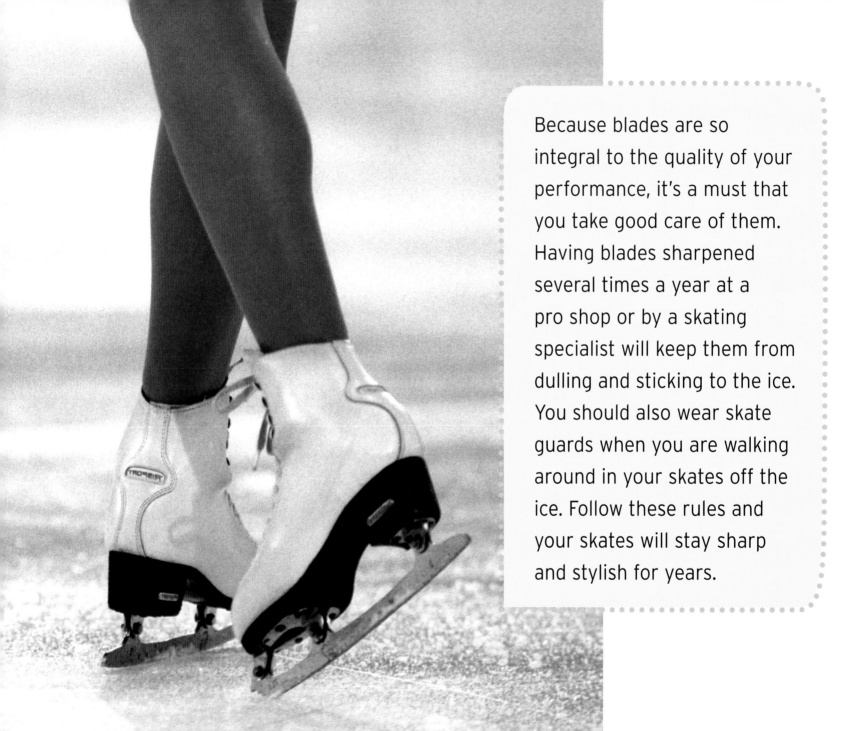

Because blades are so integral to the quality of your performance, it's a must that you take good care of them. Having blades sharpened several times a year at a pro shop or by a skating specialist will keep them from dulling and sticking to the ice. You should also wear skate guards when you are walking around in your skates off the ice. Follow these rules and your skates will stay sharp and stylish for years.

The Maiden Voyage

Are you ready to make your mark on the ice? After walking around for a bit in your skates to gain your balance, you'll be ready to take your first steps on the ice. Venturing onto the slippery surface can be intimidating for beginners, so take it slow during your first time.

Walking on the ice is just like taking "real-life" steps. Standing up straight and keeping your knees slightly bent will be your ticket to the least amount of falls or wobbles.

All Tied Up

To lace up your skates, start working from the toes upward, to the top. (Make sure to pull extra tightly at the base of the ankle for maximum support.) Tie the laces in a double knot when you finish and get ready for skating greatness! (Tip: To break in your skates, wear them around the house with skate guards on or put on damp socks while wearing them the first few times, which will soften the leather.)

The Basics of Ice Travel

Once you reach the initial comfort zone on the ice, you're ready for takeoff. The next logical step from walking is to progress to a slow, graceful forward glide.

To glide, push off the ice with the outside edge of one skate, with your knee slightly bent, while your other leg leaves the ice to stretch behind you, with toe pointed outward. After gliding forward, bring your feet back together and push off with the opposite foot, repeating the process. (Hint: Your body weight should be shifted to rest on whichever foot is currently gliding on the ice.) Forward you go!

Some skaters use techniques like sculling and dipping to improve their skating abilities. Sculling involves making an hourglass shape with your skates on the ice. It helps to improve speed and balance. Dipping involves a deep knee bend and helps to improve posture and body line.

As you become more advanced, you'll learn to skate backwards and to perform crossovers, in which you round corners and increase your speed on the ice.

Safety on the Ice

Gather too much momentum or take a sharp turn, and you might find yourself face-to-face with the ice! Knowing how to properly stop can play a major role in how much control you have on the ice. When you do fall, it's a must that you know how to cushion your body in order to minimize injury.

While some beginners prefer to skate into the wall as a means of stopping, there are much less painful methods. While skating, there are three main ways to stop: the T-stop (your feet form a "T"), the hockey stop (both feet go to one side together), and the snowplow stop (your feet form a "V"). The snowplow is popular with beginners, but advanced skaters tend to choose the hockey stop. You and your instructor can determine which stopping technique is best for you.

Falling With Finesse

When first learning to skate, taking some tumbles is completely normal. Armed with the knowledge of how to fall safely and recover properly, you'll bounce back in no time.

- Bend your knees and lean forward, with hands in front of you to break the impact of the fall.

- Let your body slide across the ice to absorb the shock after you fall.

- To get up, position your hands and knees against the ground, and then raise yourself to a kneeling position. Bring one knee forward, and put your hands on it to steady yourself as you slowly stand.

Lutzes and Camels and Flips, Oh My!

Spins and jumps are largely responsible for the beauty of figure skating, inspiring awe and wonder from those who observe them. Skaters who perform these skills in competition are participating in freestyle skating, which is done solo. They are judged on speed, height, position, and difficulty level.

Edge jumps use the outside edge of the blade for takeoff, whereas toe jumps utilize the toe pick to achieve airtime. Types of edge jumps include the waltz jump, axel, salchow, and the loop. All of these jumps use only the skating foot to lift off the ice, with no assistance from the free foot. Types of toe jumps, or flip jumps, include the flip and the lutz. These jumps involve taking off on one foot and landing on the other foot.

All spins are centered on a single spot. The most common spins are the upright spin, sit spin, layback spin, and camel spin. To avoid dizziness, skaters often "spot," much like ballerinas, by picking a stationary object to fixate on while rotating.

Ulrich Salchow

Much like Axel Paulsen, Ulrich Salchow was immortalized for the jump that he created. The "salchow" has a backward takeoff, one rotation in the air, and a backward landing. A highly successful skater, Salchow snagged the World Championship title 10 times between 1900 and 1911.

It Takes Two

Pairs skating involves two partners (usually a man and a woman) who use teamwork to perform challenging skills side-by-side at a fast pace. The power of two is obvious during pairs figure skating exhibitions and competitions. Dazzling overhead lifts and gravity-defying jumps make it almost impossible for the audience to tear their eyes away.

The basis of pairs skating is an interesting blend of the jumps and spins of freestyle skating, the fluid movements of ice dancing, and the unison of synchronized skating. (Synchronized skating is a relatively recent discipline that involves teams of eight to 20 skaters performing the same choreography, with elaborate formations and visual effects.)

If you're interested in pairs skating, you'll need to find a suitable partner. When choosing a skating partner, select someone with whom you are alike in personality, height, age, and skating style.

Daring Duos

First introduced at the 1908 Olympic Games, pairs skating has its share of notable athletes and champions. Some of the most successful pairs in history with two-time gold medals include:

- France's Andree and Pierre Brunet (1928 and 1932)

- Russia's Lyudmila Belousova and Oleg Protopopov (1964 and 1968)

- Russia's Ekaterina Gordeeva and Sergei Grinkov (1988 and 1994)

When the Rink Becomes a Ring

Competitive skating inspires its participants to strive to be the best at their craft in order to earn top honors. Going this route means long hours of practice and a willingness to constantly learn new skills and routines. The rewards can include recognition from peers, a feeling of accomplishment, and a possible path toward becoming a professional figure skater.

To be eligible for major skating competitions, an amateur skater must first pass a series of U.S. Figure Skating Association (USFSA) tests, which can be taken at a member club. The type of competitive skating you want to do will determine which tests you must take. For instance, a "junior single" skater must pass only the moves and freestyle skating tests in order to compete.

In a competition, there are two events for both men and women. The technical program requires certain moves that must be executed throughout the routine, while the free skate gives skaters more freedom of choreography. Each judge gives two marks ranging from 0 to 6 (the highest) for both artistic impression and technical merit (value). Factors such as control, grace, and style play a major role in the marks that skaters receive.

Suit Up for Success

When performing on the ice rather than just practicing, you need to look the part. Competitive and professional skaters avoid bulky sweats and practice outfits. Instead, they choose glitzy, functional costumes that show off the body line.

Girls' and women's costumes are normally made up of a spandex leotard, a skating skirt with tights, and white skates. Boys' and men's costumes usually consist of form-fitting

pants, a long-sleeved shirt, and black skates. However, most costumes are far from plain and are normally covered with beading or other decoration. Sometimes they even go along with a musical theme or reflect the flag of the skater's home country. (In the past, some skaters wore such crazy outfits that in 1988 the International Skating Union passed rules about appropriate clothing!)

Although costumes are sold in skate shops and other specialty stores, most competitive skaters have their outfits specially designed and handmade to make sure they are original. These costumes often cost thousands of dollars, but there are also many budget-friendly clothing options available.

Get in Step

Have you ever admired a synchronized swimmer's perfect timing, dazzling moves, or flawless routines? Now, imagine that on ice. Synchronized skating or "synchro" as it is popularly referred to, is a form of figure skating in which performers (anywhere from eight to 20) skate in unison, performing dance routines in formation. These dances include circles, lines, blocks, wheels, and just about anything else you can imagine.

If you're interested in synchronized skating, you should know that because of its fast speeds and difficult routines, you must be a great athlete and have a good memory. Rhythm and timing are also important.

Did You Know?
Currently there are more than 400 teams competing nationwide in synchronized skating events. It is also considered the fastest growing competitive sport in the world.

Boogie Down in Blades

Ice dancing is the new kid on the block in the skating world. It was officially introduced at the Olympics in 1976. So what makes it different from pairs figure skating? Although it calls for the same grace, ice dancing is more about fancy footwork and use of music, rather than the acrobatic skills featured in figure skating. (Ice dancing pairs are not allowed to do lifts above the man's shoulders, and there are no jumps.)

Some call it ballroom dancing on ice because it uses traditional dances like the waltz and fox trot. In competition, there are three events: the compulsories (routines with required patterns and dance steps), the original dance (an original routine performed to a required tempo and rhythm), and the free dance (where skaters show off their creativity).

Did You Know?
Noted ballet choreographer Lar Lubovitch is also accomplished in the field of ice dancing. He designed routines for Olympic medalists like Dorothy Hamill and choreographed (designed the dance moves for) a televised ice dancing version of *Sleeping Beauty*.

Legends of the Ice

To cover all of the skaters who've shaped and excelled in the sport, you 'd need an encyclopedia! Here are two of the top skaters:

BRIAN BOITANO (U.S.)

Brian Boitano holds a very special place in figure skating. After winning the gold medal in Calgary at the 1988 Winter Olympics, Boitano won 10 straight competitions on the professional circuit. This caused the International Skating Union to introduce the "Boitano rule," making professional skaters eligible as "amateurs" for certain competitions. This allowed professional skaters to compete in the Olympics.

MICHELLE KWAN (U.S.)

Michelle Kwan has never won the Olympic gold, but she remains the most decorated figure skater in the history of the United States, with five World Championship titles and many other honors. Kwan became a senior-level figure skater at the age of 12. In 1997, she introduced what would become her signature move, the "change of edge spiral." She continues to skate and compete on the professional circuit.

Going for the Gold

Figure skating has a special place in Olympic history; it was the first winter sport to be included in the London Games in 1908. There are four main skating events at the Winter Olympics: Ladies' Singles, Men's Singles, Pairs, and Ice Dancing. Some of the most popular international figure skaters who have taken the gold include:

SONJA HENIE (NORWAY)

After consecutive Olympic gold glories in 1928, 1932, and 1936, Sonja Henie (right) went on to Hollywood to make films such as *Thin Ice* and *The Countess of Monte Cristo*.

SCOTT HAMILTON (U.S.)

From 1981 to 1984, Hamilton dominated the world of men's figure skating. He won 16 U.S. and world competitions in a row. In 1984, he won an Olympic gold medal in Sarajevo, Yugoslavia.

PEGGY FLEMING (U.S.)

When Peggy Fleming was 11 years old, the entire U.S. figure skating team was killed in a tragic plane crash. Her skating coach was one of the casualties. Fleming continued her coach's legacy by winning five U.S. titles, three world titles, and an Olympic gold medal in 1968.

DOROTHY HAMILL (U.S.)

Dorothy Hamill became America's sweetheart when she won the gold medal in 1976 with a string of 5.9 marks from the judges (6.0 is a perfect score).

Where the Pros Go After the Gold

After achieving competitive success as an amateur, many figure skaters go on to become professionals. This gives them the opportunity to make money, continue to do what they love, and share it with audiences.

One of the most popular professional opportunities for skaters is to star in a touring show. The most famous of these shows was the *Ice Capades*, an extravagant musical show of ice follies that debuted in 1940 and was popular for many decades. Many modern shows are patterned after it, with elaborate musical, holiday, or Disney themes.

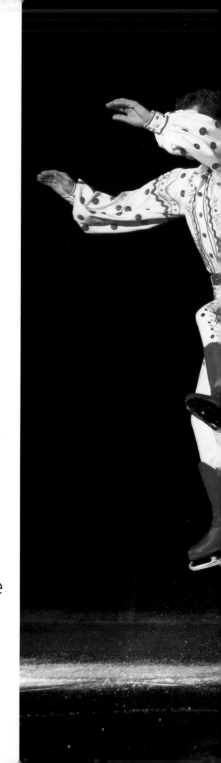

Other examples of popular ice shows include *Champions on Ice* and *Stars on Ice*, which feature former Olympians and well-known figure skaters who perform exciting choreography and their most awe-inspiring tricks. Some of the Olympians that performed in the 2005 *Champions on Ice* included Michelle Kwan, Elvis Stojko, and Irina Slutskaya.

The Jump Spin involves a backward edge take-off, full rotation in the air, and a backward edge landing.

What Happened When?

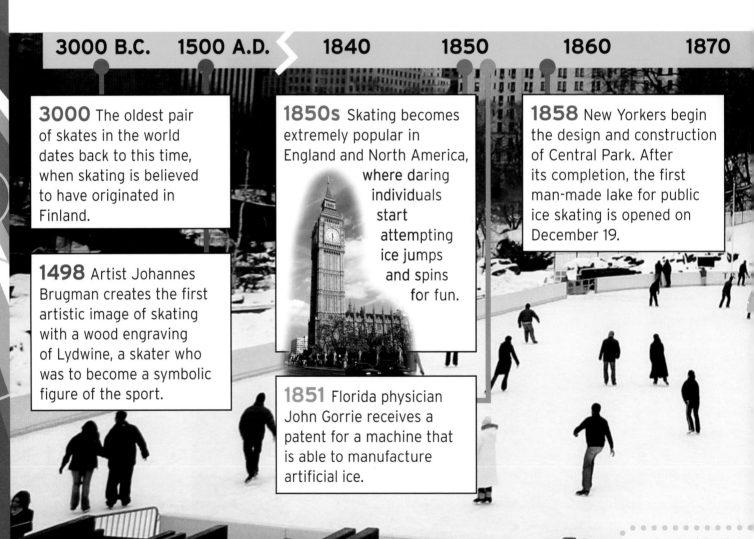

3000 B.C.	1500 A.D.	1840	1850	1860	1870

3000 The oldest pair of skates in the world dates back to this time, when skating is believed to have originated in Finland.

1498 Artist Johannes Brugman creates the first artistic image of skating with a wood engraving of Lydwine, a skater who was to become a symbolic figure of the sport.

1850s Skating becomes extremely popular in England and North America, where daring individuals start attempting ice jumps and spins for fun.

1851 Florida physician John Gorrie receives a patent for a machine that is able to manufacture artificial ice.

1858 New Yorkers begin the design and construction of Central Park. After its completion, the first man-made lake for public ice skating is opened on December 19.

Central Park, New York City

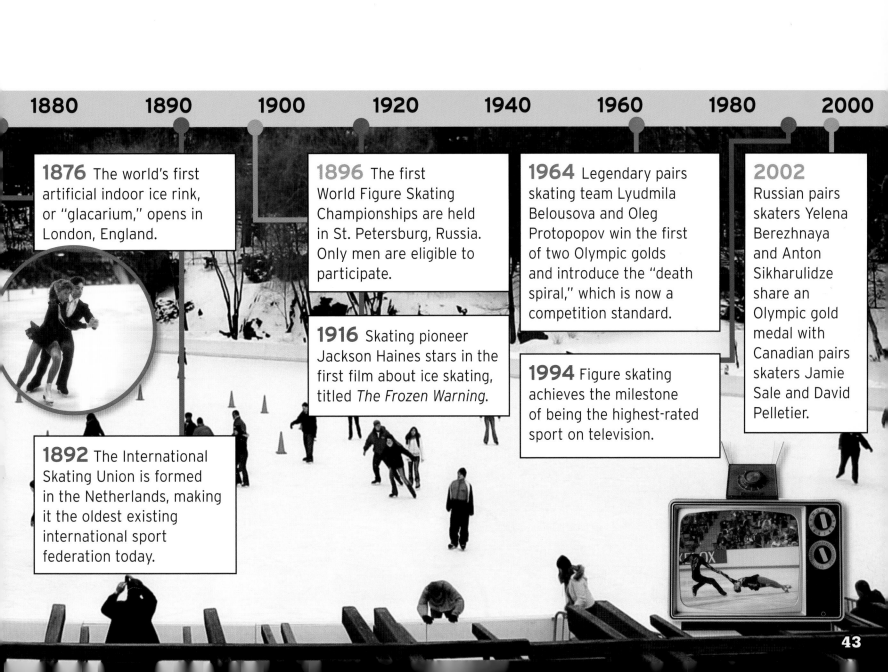

1880	1890	1900	1920	1940	1960	1980	2000

1876 The world's first artificial indoor ice rink, or "glacarium," opens in London, England.

1896 The first World Figure Skating Championships are held in St. Petersburg, Russia. Only men are eligible to participate.

1916 Skating pioneer Jackson Haines stars in the first film about ice skating, titled *The Frozen Warning*.

1892 The International Skating Union is formed in the Netherlands, making it the oldest existing international sport federation today.

1964 Legendary pairs skating team Lyudmila Belousova and Oleg Protopopov win the first of two Olympic golds and introduce the "death spiral," which is now a competition standard.

1994 Figure skating achieves the milestone of being the highest-rated sport on television.

2002 Russian pairs skaters Yelena Berezhnaya and Anton Sikharulidze share an Olympic gold medal with Canadian pairs skaters Jamie Sale and David Pelletier.

Fun Facts About Figure Skating

Canadian skater Elvis Stojko was the first to perform a quadruple jump combination at the 1991 World Championships.

In prehistoric times, hunters used skates not for leisure, but for survival. Skates helped them move around more quickly during the bri winter months and hunting season

The first skates were not made of metal, but instead from the leg bones of horses, deer, and sheep. (Skating earned its name from the Dutch term *schake*, which means "leg bone.")

Skating, in its more modern form, began in the late 1800s, when the pastime became quite popular in England.

The President's Council on Physical Fitness and Sports counts figure skating among the most vigorous activities. It estimates that a figure skater burns 384 calories in an hour.

Ice skating pairs have made magic on the big screen in movies like *The Cutting Edge* (1992) and *Champions: A Love Story* (1979).

Well-known fashion designer Vera Wang was once a competitive figure skater in the 1960s. She went on to design lavish costumes for Olympic skaters Nancy Kerrigan (right) and Michelle Kwan.

Figure skater Michelle Kwan always wears a gold dragon necklace for good luck.

Figure Skating Words to Know

alpha: a title applied to beginning figure skaters

blade: the sharp metal part of an ice skate that is used to move about on the ice

body line: the posture and positioning of your body as you skate

boot: the leather part of an ice skate that covers your foot

crossovers: skating maneuvers in which your feet cross over each other to gain speed and round corners

dipping: a skating technique that improves posture and balance

exhibition: an event in which skaters show off new routines that they plan on using in competition

freestyle skating: a type of skating performed by singles skaters that incorporates complex turns and jumps

ice dancing: a type of skating that incorporates elements of ballroom dancing and graceful movements

inside edge: the inner part of the blade that is used in conjunction with specific skating maneuvers

ISU (International Skating Union): the oldest governing international winter sport federation that oversees international competitions and events

jumps: airborne skating movements that often incorporate turns

marks: scores of merit given by judges that determine final rankings

outside edge: the outer part of the blade that is used in conjunction with specific skating maneuvers

sculling: a skating technique that improves speed and balance

skate guards: cloth or plastic coverings that are used to protect the blades when walking around in skates off the ice

skating club: an organization that provides training, competition, and social opportunities for aspiring skaters

spins: a series of rotations on the ice

synchronized skating: the newest competitive genre of figure skating that features eight to 20 skaters performing in unison

toe pick: the ridged front end of a skate that helps propel skaters into the air for flips and jumps

USFSA (U.S. Figure Skating Association): the main governing figure skating association in the United States that determines competition bylaws

Zamboni machine: a large machine that is used to clean the ice and smooth the skating surface

GLOSSARY
Other Words to Know

choreography: dance and skating movements that are predetermined and carefully created by experts

crescendo: a musical passage that gradually increases to a dramatic flourish

formation: a shape or placement of a group of performing athletes

revolution: a full turn or rotation

Where To Learn More

AT THE LIBRARY

Gutman, Dan. *Ice Skating: From Axels to Zambonis.* New York: Penguin Books, 1995.

Morrissey, Peter. *The Young Ice Skater.* New York: DK Publishing, 1998.

Wilkes, Debbie. *The Figure Skating Book: A Young Person's Guide to Figure Skating.* Buffalo, N.Y.: Firefly Books, 1999.

ON THE ROAD

World Skating Museum and Hall of Fame
20 First St.
Colorado Springs, CO 80906
719/635-5200

ON THE WEB

For more information on FIGURE SKATING, use FactHound to track down Web sites related to this book.

1. Go to www.facthound.com
2. Type in this book ID: 075651679X
3. Click on the *Fetch It* button.

Your trusty FactHound will fetch the best Web sites for you!

INDEX

ABOUT THE AUTHOR

Jen Jones is a Los Angeles-based writer who has published stories in numerous magazines. She has also written for E! Online and PBS Kids, as well as being a Web site producer for major talk shows.